Shekinah
in the
Country

"Holy persons draw to themselves
all that is earthly."

to be

"...encircled by the arms
of the mystery of God."

because

"Every creature is a glittering,
glistening mirror of Divinity."

Quotes excerpted
from the works of
Hildegard of Bingen

Shekinah in the Country

by

M.J.Nelstrum

Published by Oxbow

Copyright © 2015 M.J.Nelstrum

Oxbow ISBN – 13: 978-0692583029

Book Design and Artwork by the Author (with special thanks to Cindy and Sue who helped so often in more ways than they knew).

For my mothers:

Mary Katherine

and

Wyona Belle

The glory of God sparkling in everything

– that is **Shekinah**.

To witness the sparkling

– that is **Hierophany**.

Table of Contents

Abundance *1*

Pagans *3*
Green Tomato Relish *7*
Pumpkin Seeds *11*
The Smell of Manure *17*
The Birds Ate Our Berries *21*
I Need More *25*

Hierophanies *29*

Weeds *31*
I Noticed My Hands *33*
Monarch Butterflies *37*
Minding My Business *41*
A Sow in Trouble *45*
Ownership *51*
Baptism and Communion *55*

Transitions *59*

This Is You *61*
Shobi *65*
When Mama Died *73*
Let Me Be Dirt *77*
Planting Potatoes *79*
Now *87*

About the Author *91*

Abundance

Pagans

"...for Jews demand signs and Greeks look for wisdom..." *(I Cor 1, 22)*

The last time was 1991. The next time will be 2029. These are the rare times when the Fall Equinox and the Harvest Moon occur precisely on the same day.

This time, because it is rare and special time, because rare and special times are often sacred, because there is something in all of us that yearns for the sacred, we had a celebration, a festival, a party, a bonfire, homemade wine, hand-raised roast pig and roast goat, pickled eggs, corn cake, pumpkin and apple everything – and more – all we considered good and meant for sharing.

We had a Fall Equinox Harvest Moon Celebration Festival! (A shorter name would not have done it justice...

Someone asked if it was pagan. Someone asked if it was religious. Thankfully, those people did not come.

The people who understood that it was sacred came. The people who knew that the earth, its bounty and its fickleness, that moonlight and firelight, and pigs and apples are holy came. The people who knew that wine and food and laughter and sharing are spiritual came. The people who hear music in shouting children and night breezes and river noises came. The people who required no other explanation than the invitation to the Fall Equinox Harvest Moon Celebration Festival came. The people who knew that mutual contributions of food were only natural to the event came.

It was good and glorious fun as all such events inevitably are. We knew. We all knew. We knew what to prepare and what to share and what to do when we gathered. We knew it was everyone's responsibility to keep the wood on the fire and the kids off it. Nobody waited on anybody and everybody served everybody. Everyone was a host and everyone was a guest and no distinctions of other kinds were made.

Was it pagan?! What in the world can be meant by that?! What is pagan? Is it pagan to recognize the events of the moon and earth and stars? Is it pagan to live within the seasons? Is it pagan to gather around the stored sunlight of a blazing fire? Is it pagan to share the ease of naturally fermented wine? Is it pagan to share these things in mutual affection with one another? Please. Please tell me if these things are pagan and I will gladly claim the title.

And aren't these things what religion is supposed to be? Isn't religion supposed to be about a community of sharing? Isn't it supposed to be about the glory of the All There Is? Isn't it supposed to be a recognition that we are one with each other and all we know and the All There Is? If such a religion still exists, if such a community exists somewhere, please, please tell me where, so I can join.

Or is it more likely that the word pagan has been distorted to mean unholy and that religion has been perverted into politics? If that is the case, and it certainly seems to be, I will do my very best to keep my distance from both of them.

Because I prefer the shared joy that springs naturally from the human heart at the harvest and the changing of the season.

Because the wisdom is in the signs and the signs are all around us.

And the signs all read the same: "Come. Come glory in the All There Is."

Shekinah in the Country

Green Tomato Relish

Green tomato relish is an end of garden delight. It is a bonus, a fond farewell, a tribute. Toward the end of summer, which comes very early this far north, it's difficult to let go of a vegetable garden. It's almost as if I'm saying goodbye to a child.

The seeds, holding within themselves the promise of produce, were started indoors while snow still covered the ground in many places. After only a few days, tomato seedlings, with barely a half dozen or so leaves, already smelled like tomato plants, at least when my nose nearly touched them and I breathed very deeply. Peppers rose from the dirt still wearing seed coats as hats atop the uppermost leaves. Leeks and onions appeared as tiny threads of green, so delicate and small that it was hard to know if I actually saw them or simply hoped I did.

Hope is the essence of gardening.

It is a wonder to me year after year to see roots and shoots arise from the tiny black spheres that are onion seeds, or the flat beige ovals of tomato and pepper seeds – and all the rest –seeds – smooth, netted, nubbley, spotted, big as pencil erasers, small as freckles. How is it possible for them to hold vegetables and flowers? Hope at its faintest, I carry the mindset of an amateur, or the heart of the faithless, at least in the very early spring. Every year I plant many multiples of the seeds I need, convinced that germination is a near impossibility and that I'm up against the longest of odds. And every year I am faced with hundreds of plants – numbers far in excess of my ability to get them planted – and so to be given away, even forced upon, anyone who happens by. And every year, because they're alive, because they beat the odds, I plant more seedlings than I intended, expand my garden, find new little spots to cultivate.

Every year the seedlings are hope actualized.

Many weeks of tending the infant plants brings me only to a question: Is it time? Is it time for them to make their way in the big outdoors, subject to strong winds, flood or drought, late frosts, the competition of weeds, the predation of bugs. Are they big enough to survive, strong enough to thrive? Is it time? There comes a moment, or so it seems to me, when the plants themselves declare their readiness to depart their indoor confinement. They seem to droop a bit, to stall in their growth, to search for real sunshine, to thirst for real rain. And so. One by one I take them in hand, settle them into small hollows prepared for them, snuggle rich soil around their roots, whisper a prayer, and walk away, leaving them to nature.

Or so it seems. Because I'm not long in returning to their sides, checking for sunburn and water needs, keeping an eye on the weather. It is astonishing how they flourish – and how quickly! By the end of July, I can no longer keep up with them. I have produce in abundance. I harvest, can, freeze, pickle, ferment. The chickens are dizzy from scraps and peelings and seeds. I have to weave my way through a half dozen five-gallon buckets of produce on my back porch. I try to push vegetables on the folks who were too smart to accept seedlings – those having accepted seedlings struggling with their own abundance.

Abundance is the lesson of gardening.

Overwhelming abundance. Why am I surprised? The seeds germinated beyond my hopes, the plants bore fruit beyond my expectations. Gardening allows me to be my best, most generous self. I find myself thinking, "I wonder who might enjoy fresh tomatoes." I find myself offering my seeds, my seedlings, my vegetables, my labor as they should be offered – as if they were never really mine at all, as if nature itself was doing the giving. As it does.

Very early in the year, too early every year, frost warnings begin to appear in the weather forecast. The wind carries hints of fallen leaves behind the smell of tomato vines. It is too soon for it to be over and I struggle against it. I protect the plants, now seeming vulnerable and defenseless again, with tarps and blankets and prayer for one night, then two, until autumn becomes plainly inevitable.

I cannot face the waste – waste, the offspring of ingratitude. So, as women for generations have done, I pick the tomatoes, still hard and green, the peppers, both sweet and hot, the cabbages and onions unfazed by early frosts, indeed, whatever remains of the garden. The ratios of one vegetable to another are not important and vary from year to year. They are chopped to tiny bits, stirred together, brined, herbed and spiced, and preserved as relish – as a taste of summer on hot dogs, on grilled cheese sandwiches, in chicken salad – as a reminder of warmth and sunshine through the cold dark winter.

Green tomato relish: a reminder to hope in springtime, to revel in the promise of abundance and warm sunshine, to reverence the wonder of seeds and tomatoes.

Pumpkin Seeds

It was processing pumpkins that made me start thinking.

I had picked them about a month ago, placed them strategically along my sidewalk, on my porch, amidst cornstalks and pots of mums, among winter squash and fallen leaves, to enjoy the collage of autumn as I worked outdoors on the last of my garden chores. Now, having survived a few light frosts, bearing on their bottoms scrapings from tiny teeth of tiny rodents, and facing the prospect of a hard freeze, it was time to bring them in.

They were beautiful. Intensely orange, deeply ribbed, slightly flattened orbs, heavy with promise. In this case, the promises related to pumpkin pies, pumpkin breads, and an experimental pumpkin wine. Plus the seeds.

Having purposefully chosen open pollinated varieties when I ordered seeds, I had intended from the beginning to save them from my most successful plants for use next spring. I think it's particularly useful to acquire seed saving habits this far north. If a plant does well in our cool weather and short season, it has genetics worth saving!

And in the case of pumpkin seeds, being worth saving is especially important because retrieving and cleaning the seeds is not as easy to do as it is for the majority of garden vegetables, flowers, and herbs. Getting into a large pumpkin takes strength and nerve and a very large, very sharp knife. (I found myself wishing I had a machete. And body armor.)

From an aesthetic perspective, pumpkins are not nearly as beautiful on the inside as they are on the outside, but they are at least as wondrous. Most of the space inside a pumpkin is filled with a tight snarl of stringy fiber surrounding a shocking abundance of seeds. But the seeds don't appear numerous at first glance, hidden as they are by the dense web of fiber.

The best tool for removing the seed-filled mesh from the meaty walls of the pumpkin turned out to be a sturdy shallow ice cream scoop. I transferred all the insides, now becoming unraveled, to a dishpan where they could wait till the pumpkin proper was in the roaster. With the first scents of roasted pumpkin escaping the roaster lid, I began to disentangle seeds from the stringy goop. It was slow going. And there were a lot of them. My mind began to wander.

Maybe I haven't watched enough really good ones, but science fiction movies, especially the ones with extraterrestrial creatures, strike me as exceptionally devoid of imagination. Here, on our "home planet", the most readily recognizable species, including are own, share a common characteristic: bilateral symmetry.

Nearly everything the average person could name, including the average person, from butterflies to lizards to elephants, if creased down the middle (between the wings or along the backbone or some such place) would have two halves that fold together and overlap one another. This is true even of starfish if creased along the correct line (although biologists would disallow this classification because five such creases would be possible and they permit only one in their system). It is also true of every imagined space alien. Are no other shapes or symmetries possible?

One of the tools in the giant science toolbox, refers to this crease as a mirror plane, meaning that the two halves on either side of the plane reflect one another. The same tool, group theory, provides descriptors and categories of various shapes (geometries) based on symmetry elements. (Note: This is the tool a chemist would grab from the box. A biologist would grab a different tool, taxonomy, and require that the crease be in a specific location: the sagittal plane. The chemist's tool in this case is less limiting and therefore more appropriate to the thoughts at hand.) Although group theory limits the number of types of shapes (called point groups), too, it certainly includes more possibilities than the single variant with the single symmetry element of bilateral symmetry. Theoretically then, many more shapes are possible. Why then, could life not assume one of these shapes?

Group theory includes symmetry considerations for "objects" possessing more than three dimensions, and these are mathematically described in much the same manner as three dimensional objects are. Why then, could life not span multiple dimensions?

However, from this it should not be taken to mean that scientists are necessarily more broadly imaginative than the average person. In fact, in some ways, many scientists become tightly bound to what they know and consequently less open to the purely imagined. In this respect, science and science fiction are more closed to creative possibility than it at first appears. When scientists consider extraterrestrial life, they are not bound by symmetry limitations as entertainment producers are. They are bound by water. For them, the search for water on celestial bodies is exactly equivalent to the search for life. They state emphatically that water is an absolutely essential need for life. And it is. Here. On the home planet. Where "carbon based" life forms are the only known form. But why should this be?

Certainly, there are reasons – chemical reasons, biological reasons – that underpin the scientific belief that water is a precondition for life. But it should be born in mind that all these reasons are based on our experience here, on knowledge developed here. Is there nowhere else? Might other rules apply in these places?

What occupies those other dimensions? What are the rules within the "there" that is likely not even a "there" in the way our three-dimensional experience and imagination would understand it?

Surely, such phenomena, such experiences, are not bound by a few shapes and restricted by a single inevitable requirement. May we be allowed to think on the possibilities? Might we be the better for it?

With my hands immersed in a mixture of pumpkin seeds, tangled fiber, and water, I remembered a fragment of a quote I'd stumbled across twice in a single week, an echo, of incense scented dimly lit places: "...in whom we live and move and have our being..." It is a quote from the liturgy, if you like, or from the New Testament, if you like, or from a Greek poet, if you like (the latter representing the first expression of this thought fragment). It echoed from all three sources for me.

Christianity, in some ways, can be a very self-absorbed perspective, worrying as it does about the salvation of single souls, and its emphasis on looking within ourselves to search for God, and then to look in other people to find God there as well. Indeed it can be valuable and enriching to see ourselves as holding God within us, bound in our bilateral, water-sustained bodies. But what if God is bigger? (And as God, mustn't that be the case?) What if God is not within us, but we are within God? What if it is true that we live and move and have our being within an unimaginable infinitude of All-There-Is? An infinitude not only beyond shape and matter, but beyond gender, beyond number, beyond mathematics and common experience.

What if even the word "within" has meanings that are beyond our comprehension?

It is not as if we are without hints. Mathematics signals possibilities we can't envision. Processing pumpkins prods our thinking.

Within the pumpkin, within the shapeless tangle of pumpkin fiber, within each uncounted pumpkin seed, there most certainly exist an infinitude of pumpkins.

The seeds are within the pumpkin. And the pumpkins are within the seed.

Even without abandoning bilateral symmetry and the water imperative, the possibilities stagger the imagination – well beyond the beautiful collage of autumn, beyond pies, breads, wines, and seeds. Beyond bilateral symmetry and water.

The Smell of Manure

There's so much of everything here: vegetables, herbs, weeds, berries, bugs, noise, birth, mud, manure, mosquitoes, babies, work, expectations, disappointments, bewilderment, and awe. It is, at one and the same time, turmoil and peace. It is life writ real.

Sunburned and rain soaked, sweltering and bone trembling cold. Sweet breezes and rainbows. Livestock looking to me for care, plants begging for freedom from competition, the weight of sickness and health, life and death upon my head, I am alternately exhilarated and exhausted.

It's not that I know no other life than the farm. I do. It's just that I'm my best self here, my most aware, most open, most grateful. Perhaps I'm one of those people who just doesn't "get" life unless I'm nearly drowning in it. Or maybe I am simply blind to it everywhere but here. I only know that I need to be close to dirt – not the earth, in the way that poets think – but dirt, under the fingernails, coating the hands, rubbed onto the nose, drifted into the hair, caked onto the knees, clinging to the shoes, dirt.

I think different parts of the country, even different parts of the county, smell different; and I think it's because of the dirt: clays and loams and sands telling the ground down ground up centuries old history of the place. It's in the smell, the feel, the look, even the taste of the dirt. Enriched by manure or decades of fallen leaves, impoverished by overgrazing, overplanting, over-chemicaling.

Although the musty forest floor dirt begotten of rotted leaves is a close second, my favorite dirt to inhale is laced with manure. There is a sweetness in the smell of manure. Really. It is not offensive except to those who have allowed childish mental squeamishness to cloud what their senses try to tell them. Even before my sight can tell me, my nose informs me what life forms occupy a dwelling or pasture. Cows, pigs, sheep, rabbits, chickens all leave distinctive scent markers about where they live and eat, mostly in the manure. It is a tiny clue, an insight into the richness of life for a dog, who knows so much after a sniff or two, and yet feels no need to classify smells into categories of good and bad, a dog who breathes without giving judgment.

I have rubbed my nose and cheeks and chin onto the bodies of baby lambs and rabbits and goats as I held them, taking for myself the warmth and innocence, the freshness of life, sitting in the straw or on a bucket, and somehow I am heartened and renewed and I discover myself to be smiling.

And so it is, too, with weeding herbs. I take on the smell of anise hyssop, oregano, dill, meadow clary, and rosemary. The bumblebees follow me away, mistaking my scent for the real thing, for a moment I am delightful to the senses of an insect. It pleases me, but it is no less than I deserve – raking and weeding, shoveling, hauling, and digging manure as I have.

Of course, it can be argued that I have already received many hundreds of times over what I deserve. In this perspective, it has been a tiny amount of planting and cultivating, stewardship and care, that has yielded more vegetables than I can eat, more seeds than I can plant, more meat, eggs, milk, more wool, more fruit, more honey than I can use. And I am afforded the superfluity that begets instinctive sharing with others, fragrant offerings of love and praise and wonder and joy, incense that rises to the divine.

And all of this is showered upon someone who looks a little old, seems kind of dirty and smells faintly of manure.

Shekinah in the Country

The Birds Ate Our Berries

The birds ate our service berries again. It was a good year for berries and the bushes were covered – first by creamy white blossoms, then tiny green berries – growing, softening – colors intensifying to bright reds and finally deepening to dark blues and purples. It was an evolving vision of delight alongside our pathway to the vegetable garden. Now only green leaves remain on the canes.

When I was a little girl my daddy told stories about his time in Korea. Marine Corps culture and a country ravaged by war left a psyche forever scarred, a world view both enamored by power and horrified by devastation. What he was like before this experience is impossible for me to know; but I am sure that what remained was neither whole nor wholesome.

As with many children of that time, my brothers and I were required to clean our plates before we could be excused from the table. It was as if my daddy believed that if we ate everything set upon our plates, the hunger and despair he saw in Korea would be somehow mitigated – lessened, repaired, erased – kept distant from his own door, table, plate.

For her part, my mama took his too few dollars and made them stretch to feed our family of six. We had a cow for milk and butter; pigs for ham, bacon and pork chops; chickens for eggs and Sunday dinners. Nothing was wasted. She canned green beans and corn and tomatoes and peaches. She cooked and sweated through the sultry summers; and we had enough to eat year round.

We did not know hunger. We knew dominance. He must have sought to teach us about need and waste. Instead we learned about fear and violence – as his punishments could be quite severe.

To read or watch the news is to be made painfully aware that hunger, indeed starvation, are pervasive in the world. War and famine deprive many millions, perhaps billions, of sufficient food to sustain life and health. The kind of devastation that horrified and scarred my daddy more than fifty years ago persists today.

Despite my daddy and the evening news, I allowed the birds to take my service berries. Again. Truth to tell, they got most of my raspberries, too.

This is not the first year my potential harvest has been squandered. If I am honest, I must confess that it will likely not be the last.

Over the past several years, we have planted, pruned, cultivated, and cared for strawberries, raspberries, grapes, currants, gooseberries, josta berries, honey berries, blueberries, and service berries. These have grown into productive maturity. They are beautiful to behold in the growing season – from pale green bud to red-gold leaves – with berries and without. The berries themselves are bursts of sunshine on the tongue – each carrying a unique sweetness and fragrance. More than sustenance, they are the elegance of nature, tiny jewels of exquisite delight.

The abundance is staggering. What is one to do with it? Once we have eaten our fill of fresh berries, frozen quarts of berries and gallons of juice, made more jams and jellies than we can eat in a year, have fermented enough wine to keep us in jovial spirits for the foreseeable future, and shared our good fortune at every opportunity – what then?

In appearance, Cedar Waxwings are birds of gentle loveliness, adorned with crest, mask, and the colors of a muted autumn. They live on berries. Mostly, I believe, on my berries. Sometimes I feel in a race with them to get the berries before they do. Other years – those of greater busyness or distraction – I surrender the berries to them.

For many years I viewed the latter as unconscionable waste. The berries, on my plate – so to speak – never made it to my mouth. What would my daddy think? I made little effort to preserve every last bit of harvest. What would my mama think? Inundated with the grimmest specters in the news, what do I think?

I think greed is the child of fear and want is the child of war. I think nature is the mother of abundance. And I think no one is hurt by sharing the bounty with all living things. The Cedar Waxwings ate our service berries again.

I think that's fine.

I Need More

In the midst of unfathomable abundance, here where life moves in hyperbole, where millions of plants beget billions of seeds, where food is produced in quantities beyond our ability to consume it, where there are more creatures, more colors and sounds and smells than can be taken in, still less fully appreciated, even here I live with a hunger, a craving that is never satisfied.

Memories of moments plague me with intense need for more.

I remember a moment in summertime. I had been mowing and stopped for a break. Perhaps I was stretching my back or my neck, perhaps I was trying to get a sense of how much sunlight remained of the day. I don't recall. What I do remember is looking toward the forest that surrounds us on all sides.

I remember the treetops – pointed deep green spires of firs and spruce, softer silhouettes of pines – leaves of lighter green – maples, ash, and oak – rounded tops held open by dark gray limbs. Indeed, as poets say, the trees touched the sky, the sky bluer than my mama's eyes. Touched, not mingled, blue and greens distinct – intimate but separate – streams of white clouds, as witnesses and participants to this moment, spoke to me, recognized me as part of the magic of the forest and the tree-touched sky.

The magic. Part of the magic, the more, the sacred and the holy, the timeless and the good. I felt it. I knew it. I was one with the All-There-Is – in all consciousness, in deep and profound awareness. In the beautiful abundance of perfect peace. Seconds only. It could not have been longer. And it was gone. Over.

But it has happened many times.

I have laid down upon the grass in the open – closed my eyes, seen sunshine even so, and felt it bake into my bones, arms thrown out to either side, feeling cool grass and soil, hearing birds and bugs, sinking into the very earth, and once again taken up and taken into the wonder, the beauty, the abundance of it all.

Leaned against a giant trunk, breathing into myself fresh pine and rotten leaves, breathing the incense of running river water, the forest breezes in my lungs and upon my face, knowing the forest as home in the way deer and porcupines and a hundred, hundred other beings do, then, too, it has come.

It is not at home only, not only in creation, but also in the created. I have heard it in music, seen it in art, read it in books. I have felt it in supermarkets and parking lots, carried in those rare smiles and faces of those who are holy and don't know it.

And even in my bed at night, or amongst the livestock at chore time, or any of all the ways I spend my nights and days – it has come upon me – surrounded me, permeated me, made me whole – and made me hunger for more.

How many of these moments have there been? Too many to remember. Too few to feel filled. More. I need more.

I cannot call these moments to myself, I cannot create them of myself, even with concentrated effort, conscious awareness, practiced meditation, fervent prayer. These moments come when they come – and they go too quickly. Elegant gifts for the soul, to the soul, of the soul, they are peeks at the something more. What? What more? What else is there? What comes next?

More. There is more. There will be more.

So, here, in the abundance all about me, I starve for the more – though I suspect I am one with it even now.

Shekinah in the Country

Hierophanies

Shekinah in the Country

Weeds

Slowly. It is disappearing slowly. People tend not to notice a disappearance when the disappearing goes slowly. Sometimes they don't notice even when it's gone.

In the wild places, the open places, the forested places, along the roadsides and pathways and ditches, there used to be a myriad of plant life. There were plants with hairy stalks and plants with hairy flowers. Some had woody stems or fleshy roots or leaves the size of dinner plates. Cousins of orchids and chrysanthemums and even apple trees, country cousins they were, growing where no one would think to plant, where the soil was too poor or the sky too shady.

In those days people lived with the land as opposed to on it and the plants were viewed as friendly things, as helpers and companions. Some were known to give the heart ease, some in a physical sense and others in an emotional sense. There were plants considered a woman's special friend, helping her in her labors. Plants were used to dye wool and hair and faces. They were used in teas and tinctures, salves and perfumes.

Where are they now, these friends and helpers and makers of joy and rest? Why, they have been renamed, of course. They have been lumped together into a single category. Those that bloomed only after sunset and those that bloomed only before, those whose flower lasted a single day and those whose blossoms graced the entire summer season, the prickly and the smooth, the tiny and the massive, all viewed with an eye that saw them as indistinguishable, one from another.

With physical attributes indistinguishable, their hidden virtues were rendered immediately invisible. They became, in the eyes of those who could not see, useless. If they were useless, they must necessarily be valueless. Once valueless, they became nuisances. Now nuisances, they had to be eradicated.

The wealth and wonder of plant diversity, the pharmacopeia of native peoples and those who lived with the land, the simple substances that graced tables and clothing and faces, that delighted palates, noses, eyes, and fingers, have been stripped from our midst.

Instead of prairies, we have cultivated fields. Instead of forests we have tree plantations. Instead of pathways, we have mown right-of-ways. Instead of cottage gardens, we have great swathes of uniformly green lawns interspersed with ovals of showy cousins that require unnatural and unholy care.

Because all the rest, all the myriad things that grow out of rows and indistinguishable, all these have been deemed weeds and they are being eradicated.

And a weed killer is simply a killer.

I Noticed My Hands

The very last of the garden was harvested, just before a killing frost took everything. Tomatoes that would never be allowed to ripen, peppers that would be left to shrivel, cabbages came later than those used for homemade sauerkraut, the last of the cucumbers, summer squash, and anything else that might be minced or ground, were tossed into the biggest bowl I own. Working from a generations old recipe, more faded than my photographs, I drained the first brine rinse from a couple gallons of minced onions, cabbage, peppers, cucumbers, and green tomatoes, holding the vegetables back into the bowl as the brine ran through my fingers.

Then something odd happened. I noticed my hands. They were purple.

The color, in and of itself, was not remarkable given that I had made mixed berry jelly the day before. Instead, the color only evidenced the fact that my hands had been intimately involved with the berries and alerted me to the fact that my hands were intimately involved in food again today.

I could have dumped the vegetables into a large colander, allowed the liquid to drain away, poured the vegetables back into the same bowl, or another one, and added the herbs, spices, and pickling syrup required for the next step. I'm sure there would have been less residual brine in the mixture if I'd done it that way. But I didn't. In fact, it hadn't even occurred to me to do it any way other than to hoist the bowl with my left arm and use my fingers as a permeable dam. Then I saw them – my hands, my purple hands, were in the food. The current situation, and a lifetime of habit, were instantly obvious: I have my hands in the food all the time!

Amongst my old family photographs – older and more faded than the handed down instructions for green tomato relish – I have one of my grandma – her hair tied up in a kerchief, sitting on the ground in her backyard under her clothesline, peeling potatoes for supper. My Aunt Dotty, hair done up in pin curls, is sitting near her, and they appear to be deep in conversation. I have another photo of my great-grandma coming in from the garden with a basketful of green beans. She is squinting, grimacing, into the sun, undoubtedly hot and sweaty in her full length dress and apron. I treasure these photographs – lovely and warm, full of sunshine and food and family.

In those days, no one worried about "germs". No one imagined that viruses or bacteria or fungi lurked uninvited in vegetables – so there was no need to consider what might be used to kill them. No one thought about Clorox or Lysol or disposable gloves. Those days are gone – gone as surely as my great-grandma, my grandma, and my Aunt Dottie.

We've become terrified murderers, wanton killing mobs – the good and the bad without distinction wiped out – scourges of nature in search of the sterile. Sterile. Lifeless. Exactly the same – definitions of one another. Germs (as nebulous and useless a word as "weeds") have become the enemy.

It is all very wrong. Without bacteria and fungi, we must forego cheese and sauerkraut, wine and beer, and a hundred other delights mankind has known for millennia. We also witness the deterioration of our own health without the gut flora that assist our nourishment and immune system.

If we can, for a moment, put the fear, the Chlorox, the Lysol, the disposable gloves away – if we can step back and push the "ewww" factor away – if we can, for only a moment, embrace the wholeness of life, the entanglement of life forms, the interdependency of species too small to see with those we hold magnificent – if we can see the inherent beauty, not only in horses and roses, but also in bugs and dandelions – then we would see that the world is not a dangerous place. We would seek intimacy rather than war.

And we would see that it's not only okay to have our hands in our food, but that it is one of the myriad ways to be intimate with our world. We would make green tomato relish using our hands to hold the vegetables as the brine drains away – just like my great-grandma, and my grandma, and my Aunt Dotty did.

And if our hands are purple? Well, so much the better.

Monarch Butterflies

I don't know what lives here. I don't know where they come from. And I don't know where they go. There are worlds here and I am ignorant of most of them.

A few years ago I planted butterfly weed near the steps of my front porch. They weren't the hybridized, bred-up, domesticated version with the neon orange blooms – not that I have anything against those varieties. It was more a matter of money. Rather than buy a potted version from the local nursery and transplant it, I bought a packet of seeds from a company that specializes in herbs. The upside is that it was a much cheaper way to go. The downside was that, at the time, I didn't have any idea what the plant would eventually look like. I simply hoped that it would be something fragrant and beautiful for me to enjoy from my porch.

It is unimpressive – as the non-hybrid, non-bred-up, non-domesticated versions of ornamental plants generally are. I've looked it up. (Some might argue that I should have done that earlier in the process.) The plant

I have is a healthy form of spindly, tall, sparsely leaved. But it is vigorous. The blooms tend toward a deep pink, almost purple. I couldn't decide what to do with it – let it grow or dig it up and plant something more beautiful.

One midsummer day, when the plant was about two years old, I noticed that it was covered by yellow and black striped caterpillars. It was as if they had come overnight. Dozens of them, perhaps a hundred or more, climbed on stalks and leaves. I am ashamed that I didn't know what they were, that my granddaughter had to tell me they were the caterpillars of monarch butterflies. She asked if she could have two of them to watch them turn into butterflies.

She gathered leaves, stuffed them into a quart canning jar, covered the jar with hole-punched plastic wrap secured with a metal ring, gently invited two caterpillars inside, and took the jar home.

Within two or three days, my butterfly weed was completely decimated by the caterpillars. Not a leaf remained. The plant did, however, in what appeared to be a desperate desire to propagate, produce seed pods at the top of each stripped stem. The decision had been made for me, or so it seemed. The butterfly weed had been destroyed by caterpillars. I could replace it the following spring.

Springtime in the country is very busy and issues that serve only aesthetics are often pushed back till later. In the crush of lambing season, starting seeds for the vegetable garden, and preparing for new baby chicks, I had completely forgotten my plan to find something nice to replace my butterfly weed. Instead, the butterfly weed had taken care of itself. It had come back from its original roots in its own full and spindly vigor. And it had spread, casting its seeds over a wide area with a reproductive efficiency that undoubtedly had earned it its name – a weed. And it was as such that I viewed it then.

Until the monarch butterflies came back. Until it was eaten down to stubs by caterpillars. Again. I didn't dig it up and I didn't pull it up every new place it appeared. I have been rewarded, or perhaps schooled. Year after year, the butterflies and the caterpillars have returned.

But there has been a disturbing trend. Every year there are fewer. This year I saw fewer than ten caterpillars amongst all the places I have left for them. Where have they gone? What happened?

I don't know the specifics, and maybe no one does. But I'm willing to bet that somewhere along the way, someone, or many someones, someones like me, believed that the earth was meant to grow things for themselves, nourishing things, fragrant things, beautiful things – and that if growing things failed to meet those standards, the standards of serving human someones, they served no meaningful purpose at all.

But there are worlds around us, worlds of other living things, of other purposes, of different beauties. How selfish and ignorant we have been!

Butterfly weeds were never intended to ornament a porch. Butterfly weeds weren't even intended for me. Butterfly weeds were intended for the butterflies. And the world they inhabit.

This is the important part: the butterflies and I must share the same world. Our worlds are settled in upon one another, more than touching, more than overlapping.

I have a photograph of my granddaughter, sticky traces of chocolate ice cream on her lips, sitting with her legs beneath her, looking down at her fingers where two magnificent monarch butterflies cling in the moments before they are set free. There is such fragility and sweetness there – my granddaughter so young, learning that living things must be handled gently. I cannot help but wonder if my granddaughter's granddaughter will see the world of monarch butterflies and their weeds settle in upon her own world.

Even now, I don't know what lives here. I don't know where they come from. And I don't know where they go. There are worlds here and I am ignorant of most of them. But I have learned that I must tread gently upon the world I see, lest I harm the worlds I don't.

And I pray the monarch butterflies find their way here again.

Minding My Business

Just before the Fall Equinox, just before the Harvest Moon, during that small window of time when the sunshine remembers summer's warmth and the breeze predicts winter's chill, at the time of day when sunset gold halos the high and narrow spaces, while all else becomes blue-gray silhouette, in that moment between outright busyness and oblivious sleep, in that timeless space between times, I sat my weary worried self right down on the hay covered ground and leaned back against the giant round bale in its midst. I don't know if my eyes were opened to take in the All-There-Is around me, or if they were closed because such visions don't require sight at all. The ewes crunched tufts of dried grass pulled from the bale, circled it looking for better leafier bits, smelled me (and I them), stepped over my legs, continued their business.

And what is the business of a ewe in autumn? What is the business of a ewe at any time? Or the heifer in the next pen? Or the rabbits, or goats, or pigs, or poultry? What is the business of this livestock, of these animals, under my stewardship? Or the animals that are under no one's stewardship? What is their business? What is my business?

I worry about my business. I spend a good part of each and every day worrying. What will happen to the price of hay if there isn't enough rain? What will happen if there is too much rain to get the hay in? How much hay will I need? How will I pay for it? Which ram should be mated with which ewes? Will it frost tonight? Should I figure out what to do with green tomatoes or wait and hope they have a chance to ripen? Will my mortgage company finally understand they've screwed up my property taxes again? What will happen to tax rates if the frontrunner gets elected? What will happen if he doesn't? Will I ever be able to retire? Will I be able to afford to eat when I do? Is there a God to cry to? What happens when I die? What happens when anyone dies? Is there a God to go to? Is there a "there"? It is a life paralyzing spiral of "what if's" and "should I's" and "how can I know for sure". It is exhausting and useless. Everyone knows it and everyone does it anyway.

Yet, very slowly, it all melts away sitting and leaning on hay amongst the ewes. The part of my head that spins with questions and quests coasts to a stop. My heart takes on the rhythm of cud-chewing sheep. It is a rhythm I seldom adopt but that is nonetheless deeply familiar. It is the rhythm of sheep and ravens and grass and seasons. It is the beat of a thousand, thousand millennia. It is the single stroke of the now. It is the rhythm of the All There Is.

It is the All There Is, the everything that ever was, the everything that will ever be, everything our minds will ever know, everything our hearts will ever feel, every experience of every being that has lived or will live – all that, and more. It is all that, and more, wrapped in the instant of the everlasting now. It is the union of all life and being. It is part of who I am when I am unaware. It is all of who I am when I stop to breathe and know and feel the single stroke of its rhythm.

So, in the hay amongst the ewes, in the autumn of the year, and the twilight of the day, in that space and time when space and time dissolve, I felt myself once again to be taken up into the All There Is.

And that is what I know of the uselessness of worry, the God to cry to, and the place where the dead may rest. I know the single everlasting stroke of now and that I am encompassed by it.

And my business is to remember this rhythm.

Shekinah in the Country

A Sow In Trouble

Newborn animals, at least all of them I've ever seen, are precious in their tiny wholeness and their vulnerability. There is a sweetness to each and every one of them. Surprisingly, this is most true of piglets.

Even after seeing dozens, maybe hundreds, of litters of new baby pigs, it remains a wonder to me how mamas who are so big can tend to babies who are so small. Piglets typically weigh about three pounds each, and their mamas can weigh as much as five- or six-hundred pounds. It is this fearsome difference in size that has caused one of the most inhumane practices in the swine industry: farrowing crates.

I like to think the original intent of farrowing crates was a good one – to save more babies from being crushed when their mamas lie down to nurse. This is exactly the problem that farrowing crates were designed to solve. And they do! A farrowing crate is a sow sized rectangle of heavy metal tubing of such dimension to hold the sow facing a single direction, unable to turn around, or move forward, backward, or sideways. She has but two options: she can stand up and she can lie down.

It is the lying down that is key. Because the width of the crate is only inches wider than the sow herself, she must go down on her front knees first, then fold in her back legs. Once she has lowered herself to her belly in this way, the lowest bar of tubing on the crate is high enough to allow her to roll to her side, exposing her teats for her babies to nurse. Lying down in this fashion is very slow for a sow and gives her piglets time enough to escape being crushed. And it is quite true that there is no way to "un-crush" a three pound piglet laid on by a sow more than a hundred times its size. It is simply dead and there is no way of going back from that.

Worst of all, there are the rare sows who savage their young – killing or even eating them. Farrowing crates prevent this disaster as well.

Even so.

I hate farrowing crates. I've never permitted one on our farm and I don't buy breeding stock from farmers who use them. Period.

For all types of livestock, and nearly every time, birth is not the painful physical trauma it can be for women. I've heard the pain of labor for women referred to as the curse of Eve for her sin in the garden. I've also read that it may be attributed to a poorly angled pelvis – as side effect of the evolution that allowed us to walk upright. But whatever it is, and however it came about, animals are simply not burdened with it. Mostly.

When a sow farrows, she lies on her side. Following contractions that are almost imperceptible, and causing her no distress, baby pigs almost roll out, slippery, yet shockingly alert, immediately in search of their first meal. One after another they come, finding their ways to

A Sow in Trouble

the udder, climbing over one another, investigating their mama, whose snout is roughly the same size they are, until, finally, the entire litter has arrived and filled their tiny bellies with warm milk. Then they sleep, the mama still on her side, the piglets, now dry and soft as silk, in a haphazard stack against her udder. It is one of the sweetest and most comical sights on a farm.

But she can't stay there. She has to get up. She must eat, drink, defecate, move around, live. It is a frightening thing to see. The sow will grunt, scoot away from her litter, gather her back legs beneath her, roll onto her belly, and rise. She lumbers about her pen with as many as a dozen or more piglets scurrying and playing around her feet. It is very clear that if she steps on one of her brood, it will be instantly dead. But she doesn't. She doesn't step on them when she goes to the feed and water. She doesn't step on them when she goes outside or comes back inside. She doesn't step on them when she comes to the gate to see what we're doing. She just doesn't. I don't see how she avoids it. I think I'd have trouble myself avoiding that many little ones scuffling around my feet.

Several times a day, especially after she herself has eaten, the sow lies down to nurse her babies. It is as if her movements are dictated by an invisible farrowing crate. Slowly and deliberately, she descends to a prone position, front legs first, then rolls to her side. It is not a silent event. She makes soft grunting snorting calls for her babies – and her babies squeal as they run into one another, bounce from her legs and sides, jostle for best position. For all the world, it looks hopeless to the non-swine observer. It looks impossible that everyone will come out of this alive. Again. And again. Yet, they do. Again. And again.

So what's wrong with a farrowing crate, if a sow readies herself for nursing the same way with or without it?

Because that's ALL it allows her to do. It reduces her to a source of milk and nothing more.

Our sows have access to both inside and outside pens, choosing sunshine or shade as they see fit. Or warmth. During the winter we hang heat lamps in one corner of their inside quarters and pad the floor with wood chips. Sows make nests for their babies when it's cold, something they cannot do from a farrowing crate. They herd and root and nuzzle and gather their babies into whatever area they think best. Sows always think best for their piglets. Sows are far more than milk sources. They are mamas.

They are no more or less perfect than mamas of other species, including our own. Imperfection in mothering is a distressing thing to see.

This fall one of our sows began labor during chore time. This is not unusual so it is not cause for alarm. We went about our normal routine, checking the sow as we were about to leave the barn. We found her first piglet dead by her feed trough where she had bitten it clean through its skull and neck. It would be easy to condemn her as unfit, evil, a disgrace to her gender and species and purpose. It also would have been quite wrong.

My husband and I turned two five gallon buckets upside down, took our seats on them and watched the sow, now lying on her side again. We waited for the next piglet.

A Sow in Trouble

The sow strained hard, fidgeted, arose, turned around, laid down again, strained for several minutes. Just as we had decided that an internal inspection might be in order, the second piglet arrived. The sow jumped up, turned toward it, and tried to kill it as she had done its sibling. I grabbed the piglet away from her, dried it, and placed in a wood chip lined cardboard box.

It was clear what we had to do.

In the days of agribusiness and farrowing crates, a good deal of knowledge has been lost. There must have been a day when it was widely known that if a sow is stroked the length of her udder over her teats, back and forth, gently but firmly, she will settle down, lie down, and relax. Always. It must be of immeasurable comfort to them. Even if the stroking is begun while the sow is standing, in a matter of seconds, she will lie down and turn both rows of teats toward her help. And there she will stay. As long as the stroking continues.

And so we sat on our buckets, taking turns, one of us stroking the sow, the other catching, drying, and removing piglets from her pen. Difficult birth after difficult birth. Ten of them. Even as we speculated as to what internal abnormality cost her so dearly (a too-narrow birth canal? one that was tipped at a slightly wrong angle? What?), we could not help but see her pain, her distress, her confusion, her gratitude for the tiny comfort we were able to provide. Then it was over. She passed her afterbirth and began to relax. My husband continued to stroke her while I retrieved a squealing, vibrating, jumbled box of hungry piglets. One by one, we placed them at her udder, where they would scramble, search, jostle, suck, fall, try again. They climbed her legs, her side, her face, her snout. She made soft grunts and snorts.

She raised her babies, too. And with no further intervention. She was protective, careful, mindful of the minute-to-minute weather changes typical of autumn and took her babies indoors and outdoors as appropriate to the conditions. She was, in fact, an excellent mama.

She had a moment when she was overwhelmed by motherhood, when it was too much for her to endure alone, when the not quite right was rendered disastrous. Very few sows come to this moment. And even though she was a rare one who did, she was never evil or violent or a disgrace to her gender or her calling.

Imperfection in mothering is a distressing thing to see. But what if, in a mama's hour of need, instead of surrounding her with righteous revulsion and bars, we intervened with kindness? What if we helped all mamas, of all species, including our own, become the excellent mamas they were made to be?

I hate farrowing crates.

And jails.

And righteous revulsion.

I love babies.

And their mamas. However imperfect they might be.

Ownership

She comes every year. Sometimes, the dogs will bark and bounce around her in playful arcs - confused, amused, not remembering her visit last year, dogs not bound to time and season, having surrendered nature's time to human's time eons ago. Even I forget from one year to the next, recalling her only when I see her again.

She comes in early summer, around the time we first mow our yard - the grass, green, chopped to a height equivalent to her own height. She comes at a slow and steady pace, veers neither one way nor another, following a straight path to the same place every year.

I don't know what to do.

What would I have done had I known?

I'm sure when she first came to this spot, it was different from what it is now. I'm sure there was neither mowed grass nor dogs. In the long ago, this was forest - and only forest - as so much of the world used to be. Untrodden and untouched, it must have continued thus for centuries. Then, in the early 1980's, it was logged - stripped of popple, pine, and cedar.

We are, in at least so far as the abstract shows, only the fourth owners of this land. It belonged to the county, then a woman who bought it for the sole purpose of logging it, then a man who hoped to build a house but whose wife feared the surrounding wilderness. Then us.

Some loggers, whose lives are lived in forests they actually see, are possessed of a conscience. They spared specimens and spaces that, in all likelihood, the owner might not have – given that she never set foot upon her land. The loggers protected the river – leaving great swathes along it undisturbed. Many of the trees nearest the river are of such girth that two people with arms outstretched cannot join hands around them. A cedar bog remains, home to every type of wildlife that can endure the winters here, home especially to bears.

Ten years after the loggers had completed their harvest here, we bought the land. We could still see their staging areas. These are places where harvested logs were stacked, sorted, and loaded out. There were three of them, connected by logging trails to one another, one area near the north boundary, one near the south boundary, and a third near the middle of the property. Open places now, only weeds and wild raspberries, pioneer species as they are known, calling the human activity areas back to wilderness, leading a slow reversion toward used-to-be. We halted that process. We mowed where the loggers loaded. We made the logging trail a driveway. We built a house in the middle clearing.

In the short time we've been here, we've seen wolf pups, coyotes, bears, fishers, porcupines, beaver, woodchucks, eagles – and a hundred things we could not have foretold.

And the turtle.

Ownership

In the middle of our gravel driveway, just across from the second garage door, every year without fail, she comes to build her nest. The dogs alert us to her arrival. We kennel them to allow her the only measure of peace we are able to offer. Oblivious to commotion or observation, she digs a small shallow hole, and backs into it. She lingers in the area for almost a day. We have never followed her, but we assume she returns to the big pine forest and the river.

Which she owns.

And always will.

Shekinah in the Country

Baptism and Communion

Kneeling, as all suppliants do, I thought to myself, "They know I love them."

In the last hours before winter set in, in the aisle of forest between my house and our river, I sat back upon my calves and breathed in what I had done and breathed out a prayer for what I hoped it would become. Without doubt, it is an exercise in faith and patience – as all gardening is. But this time, there is an element of the sacred that is more penetrating than usual.

No tractor, no tiller, no hoe or shovel was involved. Rather, the gods of the forest were invoked, the gods of ancient peoples, of healing, of growing things, of herbs and of fungi were implored to bless my work. The sounds of the river on rocks and the winds through conifers whispered psalms of praise and supplication, of a union sought with the All There Is.

Shekinah in the Country

Many years ago strong winds uprooted a fir tree, most vulnerable of the conifers, and left behind as evidence a depression perhaps eight inches in depth, and four feet in diameter, now moss lined and leaf covered. With my bare hands, I pulled the leaves back to the rim of this shallow chalice, which I began to refill, carefully considering the needs that must be met.

I had retrieved, as nutrition, as offering from those who eat grass – well rotted manure, now faded to the color of sparrows' wings. I added, as sweetener, as offering from those who fly, or try to do so, shattered egg shells. All of these, with crumbled leaves, black dirt, humus replete with fungi, fungi as fairies to deliver every good thing to tiny seeds and baby roots – were mingled – mixed by hand, and poured into the chalice. Kneeling. It must be done while kneeling.

Smoothed over now, smaller hollows were made, and into these I placed tiny pots, sown with seeds or root buds. Reverently, the leaves, which had been edged to the rim, were returned to the chalice center, spreading a robe of forest membership upon the newcomers. Nearly and early dark, and growing colder, it was time to conclude the rite. Water was sprinkled, poured, until the newcomers were immersed in life-giving moisture.

I stood. Looking down at the new forest seedbed, the depression gone, replaced with hopes for distant spring, I acknowledged and announced my love for herbs of healing that grow in deep woodland places, and pray that I can spread their gospel.

Blessed by bloodroot and bethroot and golden seal, blue cohosh and spikenard. Blessed be the herbs and hands that heal.

Amen.

And it began to snow, flakes as white and pure as angels wings.

Shekinah in the Country

Transitions

Shekinah in the Country

This Is You

"This is you." The mantra, the chant from the East, the meditation of monks and wanderers long dead. I can imagine them walking slowly the forest paths, contemplating pebbles – this is you – fragrant humus growing green – this is you – the rising moon – this is you. Starlight and supper, breezes warm and cool, bugs and stags, droplets of mist, distant thunder. This is you. This is you. You. All of it you.

I was so taken by the imagery, the unity, the peace, the everlastingness of it, that I had it engraved on a tiny rectangle of silver, hung it from a slender chain about my wrist, and determined that I would never remove it. I craved a reminder of the living, the natural, the ordered chaos of the world, of all worlds. I felt a compulsion to dive into the mystery of the All There Is.

And I began to walk along behind the wanderers long dead – as if they lived before my eyes, as if they lived with me. This is you. And they seemed to gesture, nod, point, prod. The melting snow – this is you – the grass too cold to green – this is you...

Me.

It was the turkey that did it. I don't know what wild thing snatched it from a pen we believed secure. I don't know what feasted upon its breast and thighs. I know only the bits of bones and the bed of feathers dog-scattered throughout our yard atop the melting snow. And most unbidden, it came to me – This Is You. This? This?! This, too? Yes. Might I be allowed at least to see the feast that must have been before I am compelled to accept death's pieces? No. This is you.

This is you. This is me. It is a going out from yourself. It is a taking into yourself. I expected the former. For the latter I was ill prepared. But it cannot be otherwise. One cannot choose amongst the All There Is for the This Is You. It must be taken as it comes. You must inhale or suffocate, swallow or drown, accept everything or die of nothingness. These are the choices of the wanderers.

This is you. Bigger. Everything. All things. All There Is.

My aunt lays dying of countless tiny tumors shot through her brain. This is you. She tells me she is dying – this is you – and that she is afraid – this is you.

I tell her that it is natural to be afraid when we don't understand what our new way of being will be, that I am confident only that there will be a way of being, that it will be bigger.

And the wanderers, long dead, my aunt, soon dead, and all the living and all the dead – this is you. And that is all I understand – a tiny, hazy, fragmented understanding – of the bigger way of being and I cannot express it to her

– the tiny tumors preventing focus. So I take her into myself and I go out of myself to be with her. We will be with the silver moonlight on moving water, with horses meandering through knee-deep grass, with all those we ever loved, with all love.

The blossoms, the rage, the needs, the questions, the stars, the love, the everlastingness, the unity, all of all, everything of everything – this is you. More than I bargained for. No less than I expected. You and me. Reaching out and taking in. Feeling in me, upon me, around me, the All There Is. Unbound, unbordered, undone, un-one, only All, All There Is. This is you.

No one said there would be no tears.

Tears, too. This is you.

Shekinah in the Country

Shobi

I have heard that sharks and snakes, hippos and kangaroos grow until they die, that their size is limited only by their lifespan. I don't know if this is true of these animals, or true of other kinds of animals as well, but I know that it is true of pigs. Pigs grow till they die. I have been to many state fairs where, in the "oddity" section, there are a couple pigs on display weighing around a half ton each. They are monstrosities, barely recognizable as members of their own species. People walk by, gasp, sometimes wonder "what are those?!", stare. Protected from any type of natural death or predator, they suffer a condemnation of useless consumption and morbid curiosity. Their lives, paradoxically, are an affront to living. They deserved better.

On our own small farm, along with a handful of cattle, a small flock of sheep and goats, the poultry and the rabbits, we keep hogs. We usually have fewer than a half dozen adults and we farrow four or five litters of piglets a year. Our pigs are confined, but the pens are large, they lumber about freely, and we attend to all their needs. This appears to suit the pigs perfectly.

In fact, we are absolutely certain our pigs lead contented lives. We know this because they stay. To a person unfamiliar with pigs, they appear to be slow witted, clumsy, and physically inept animals. Nothing could be further from the truth. Pigs are surprisingly quick and agile. They are immensely powerful as well. And they are smart. Pigs can jump over fences, push through fences, root under fences, outsmart fences. I have personally witnessed each and every one of these feats.

We once owned a boar whose pen was enclosed by electric fence wire. Every morning, right after his breakfast, he would root his water trough toward the wire, short it out, and leave his enclosure. He would return for dinner. We owned a different boar who would push the fence of his enclosure apart if dinner was so much as half an hour late. He didn't go anywhere, but apparently needed an outlet for his exasperation. When we sell piglets to new owners who inquire as to what type of fencing is required for pigs, I tell them to adopt a regular feeding schedule. I tell them that pigs are the couch potatoes of the livestock world, that if they are content, they can be kept home with bailing twine for wire and popsicle sticks for posts; but if not, they can't be kept home at all. Our pigs stay home. And they're smart enough, agile enough, and strong enough that they don't have to. That's how we know they're content here.

For most of them, it is the only home they've ever known. Most of them are born here, and the rest are purchased and brought here when they are less than two months old. We save the choice gilts from the very best sows, and we purchase our boars as shoats. We have mostly Berkshires, but recently a Red Wattle was thrown into the mix. When they were each about eight weeks old, we traded a Berkshire boar for a Red Wattle boar straight across. We love our Berkshires with their beautiful wide shoulders, black all over with white points, and very pleasant but active (for pigs) dispositions. The Red Wattle was something different. He was the color of new bricks, narrower of frame looking at him from the top, and very laid back – so much so that it was sometimes difficult to determine whether he was awake or asleep, dead or alive. He worried us a little that way when we first brought him home. Sleep, in fact, became his defining characteristic – which is saying a lot for a pig. And of course, there are the wattles, those little dangles of fat that hang on each side from the area where the head meets the neck. When people notice them for the first time, they ask, "What are they for?" I reply, "Decoration."

When our new Red Wattle boar was about three or four months old, my husband and I were doing yard work when I heard a strange slowly repeating deep rasping sound that went on for quite some time. I asked my husband if he heard it and what it might be. It was our new boar – the only pig we've ever owned who snored. In proportion to his size...

We bring them feed and water, keep their pens clean, share our excess garden produce with them. (Pigs are especially fond of watermelons, cucumbers, pumpkins and the like, but then, who isn't?) You can't spend time with an animal without talking to them, and you can't talk to them without addressing them in some way, and to be addressed, they need names. Our Berkshire boars, all of them, have been called Hagar. Our Red Wattle boars are Rufus. We address all our sows, with the respect the word deserves, as Mama.

Shekinah in the Country

Standing guard over our livestock, seeing to it that all is as it should be, our second in command so to speak, is our guardian dog, a Tibetan Mastiff called Shobi (as in "King David's Friend Shobi", his registered name). I love him. Not in the way someone might love a new pair of shoes, but in the way someone might cherish a lifelong friend.

Shobi views it as his job to greet every single newborn that arrives on our farm, whether it arrives by birth or purchase. Our mamas allow this. He has slurped the noses of newborn lambs, kids, piglets, and calves. He keeps watch, on heightened alert, immediately outside, or sometimes inside, their pens for their first few days of life. If any of the grazers escape their pens, he gathers them at the gate and waits for me to open it, so everything is living within its assigned and safe borders. We live in the middle of a great swath of the Northwoods, where we have seen bear, fisher, wolves, badgers, and so on within our boundaries. We have not lost a single animal to a predator during our time here, Shobi having redirected their attention to their natural prey, also here in abundance.

On some nights, Shobi comes indoors and sleeps beside my bed. On others, presumably when threats are perceived or when the weather is particularly fine, he sleeps outdoors. We allow him to make this judgment for himself.

My brother, hearing me tell so often of Shobi's deeds, said to me, "He's your once-in-a-lifetime dog." I thought, "Yes. Yes, he is," and then, almost immediately, corrected myself, "NO! He can't be!" I realized Shobi is eight years old. Even for a breed long-lived among the large dogs, he's not as young as he used to be.

Perhaps there is an order to things that extends even beyond the obvious cycles of seasons, births, and deaths, a power that directs, protects, blesses, and teaches.

Judy, the woman I bought my first TM puppy from more than twenty years ago, emailed out of the blue, and asked if I would be interested in a puppy. How many answers to that question could there be?!

Her name is May (a call name derived from "Salome's Forgiveness", her registered name). She is typical of most puppies, in that a wake of destruction trails her, but she is different in that she is possessed of a calm gentleness, a sweetness, that peeks through at times.

Of course, given that she is just a baby, she is under Shobi's charge. He allows her to share his dinner and his bones (but only after most of the "good" has been consumed). He allows her to go nose-to-nose with our ewes and sows and nannies through the wire fence barrier, but he does not feel she's ready to go into the pens themselves. He allows her to roam the yard, yet only to a distance he feels safe. He completely banned her from one area of our clearing. Even not knowing why, we allowed him to enforce his rule, telling May that we must abide by Shobi's judgment on these issues. Only days later, a bear came up from the river bottom in exactly the area May was not permitted to go.

But they are just dogs, are they not? They do not have a person's understanding of the world and its sometimes brutal realities. Is that not so? Isn't it our responsibility to shield them from those things they cannot grasp, that they might find disturbing? If everything has a purpose, isn't this a human purpose? A part of the care of life that is incumbent upon us? These were my thoughts when I locked both Shobi and May in the garage yesterday morning in anticipation of what I knew the day would hold. They often go there anyway for the dark respite from bugs and the heat. I made them content with special treats and closed the door.

Pigs grow till they die. That doesn't mean they don't age. It just means aging doesn't stop their growth. Rufus had grown. He was very nearly seven hundred pounds. He had sired many nice litters of piglets for us, every single piglet red and decorated with wattles, despite their plain black and white mamas. We have kept several of his daughters to become future mamas themselves.

We try to use everything here. We try not to waste anything. Everything has a purpose and to deprive it of any part of that seems an arrogant sacrilege, a disrespect for its inherent value and purpose. We eat our eggs, and eventually our old hens. We save the eggshells for our garden. We put their manure on our grass. We feed them our table scraps and weeds from our garden. With chickens, it's easy. With boar pigs, it's harder.

Boars, because they need to smell a pig's version of delightful in order to inspire sows to mate with them, have what is called "boar taint". It makes their meat virtually inedible for people. It costs more to haul a boar to market than he will bring when he crosses the scale – and that was when gas was cheap! What is one to do? What is the kind thing to do?

They say that Native Americans have rituals of thanks and forgiveness when they take a life to sustain their own. I know many people who whisper prayers of praise and reverence. We do what we know to do, what seems right and sacred. Here, we say prayers to Saint Isadore, the patron saint of farmers, and to Saint Francis of Assisi, the patron saint of animals, and to Saint Joseph, the patron of our farm – and to all other saints and spirits who gaze upon us and listen to us. We pray that the animal to be slaughtered has had as good a life as we have tried to make it, that the moments before its death will be filled with calm and normality, that its death will be quick and painless, that its remains will be put to utmost use to sustain life. And then we do what we must.

Yesterday was Rufus' day for slaughter.

Because his meat would be unfit for human consumption, and because, in good conscience, we could not waste such a large amount, we had decided beforehand that his meat would be coarsely ground, frozen, and cooked as needed to be used to feed the dogs.

Clyde has slaughtered many animals for us. He takes great time and care to make sure he gets a clean kill, that he doesn't disturb the animals. He has earned my trust. Rufus died in an instant while he was having his second breakfast of the day. Clyde commented about how magnificent he'd become and yet agreed that it was time. He removed the legs from just below the back knee and made a slit between the bones of the mid-leg to insert the hooks so the carcass could be hung. He slit the carcass lengthwise down its center and we both stood for a moment, as we have done many times, to admire the beauty, the complexity of the inner body. It is, for those who can look with open mind, a wonder of textures, shapes, colors, symmetries. And then he proceeded. By the time he left, two white covered halves were in the back of his truck, and the offal, legs, and head were left neatly wrapped within the red bristle skin. The dogs, still in the garage, didn't even bark.

When my husband got the shovel to dig a hole for the remains, he let May and Shobi out of the garage. Digging a grave is hard work, and while it is not grim – our prayers sustain us – it is at least solemn, focusing as it does on the life that has ended. When he had finished he noticed May had found one of the back feet and was playing with it. We agreed to allow it.

Shobi, however, did not agree with our decision. He took the foot from May, brought it to Rufus' grave, and laid it in the center. It was as if he said, "May is just a baby, but she must learn respect." We reopened the grave enough to enclose the foot.

There is a myth among Tibetan Mastiff owners that some of these dogs carry the reincarnated souls of failed Buddhist monks. In addition, some TM's have a white mark on their chests, and this is occasionally referred to as the mark of Buddha. Shobi carries such a mark.

As for me, I don't know the meaning of any of it. I don't know if animal spirits receive our thanks and grant us their forgiveness. I don't know if saints keep special watch. I don't know if souls move from creature to creature.

I don't know. But I believe. I believe most fervently. I believe in all of it. I believe in all there is. And All There Is.

And I believe life goes on.

When Mama Died

The tips of her feet were too far back and the tip of her nose was too far forward. I could tell with my eyes closed; and closed they had to be, so I could concentrate on what I felt.

I felt the black, wet, slippery, warm, doubtful maybe that hovers between life and death – and between life and new life. The not-as-it-should-be lamb, the uncomfortable but indifferent ewe, the maybe, and me, united for a moment in the uncertain light of morning.

For animals, a borning is easier and harder than most people imagine – easier for the mama, usually, and harder for the almost born. It is a risky business.

I pushed the head back – just a bit, pulled the two feet forward – just a bit, checked for position, and when the ewe strained again, I pulled out and downward on the feet.

Then it was very quick – as it usually is if correctly done – and things are not more atangle at the outset. She was blacker than a blank spot in the universe, wet as from a baptism, and still. I picked her up by her hind feet and swung her in a wide arc like a giant pendulum – six, eight times – laid her down rubbed her vigorously all over with an old towel – picked her up and swung her again – finally draining all of her before-life out of her lungs – laid her down, rubbed her all over. Then in that moment when life hovers undecided, she breathed her life into herself, called for her mama, and tried to stand.

Her twin brother arrived unassisted a very short while later.

And I remembered seeing my mama die. I remembered hearing her die. And feeling her die.

My mama died at home, in her own bed. The day before, almost the whole day, she had what I researched and learned to know as the "death rattle". If my dad had had more sense, if he had allowed hospice help, they'd have cleared my mama's secretions, and that time would have been quieter.

When the gurgle rattle of her breathing was so loud it could be heard in another room, I went in to her room, crawled in her bed, stretched out beside her, took her hand in mind, and said, "I'm sorry this is so hard."

I'll never know if she heard me – or whether it meant anything to her if she did – but I know I meant it.

She lay a-dying and it was hard.

I don't believe in pearly gates or golden streets or robed and haloed angels. For a long time I wished I did, wished I could. But I don't. And there's the end of it.

But I do believe in something. I believe in many things. I believe in the All There Is. And I believe very strongly.

When Mama Died

We know, people know, I think it is human to know, that birth and death are paired somehow, are two sides of the same coin, are necessary to one another. Lord knows clues enough have been given. Cocoons and leaf fall and compost and a myriad of life realities all whisper the alliance. It is never over when it's over. Such a notion runs counter to the songs both sad and sweet in our own hearts.

There must be some sacred center, something for us, something between simply compost and jewelry store cities.

It must be birth.

And I think of our little lambs – warmly, wetly, safely cocooned in their mama's womb, traveling with her through the orbits of her world – alive and growing and becoming and real – in a tiny world only partly known.

They could see – but only darkly, hear – but only dimly, move – but very circumscribed, completely dependent on the world that carries them.

Then, and it is a moment, the cord snaps. And they fall untethered into a broader brighter place – where some of them breathe and some of them struggle and some of them never know that a wider life was possible.

Is that so for my mama? Did she gurgle and struggle and finally find a brighter broader world? We know there are more colors than our eyes can see. Can my mama see more colors now? We know there are more sounds than our ears can hear. Can my mama hear them now? Is she in a place that isn't a place, but more a community, more a union? Is she a part of something bigger and yet very much herself? Did she become one with the All There Is? Can she hear me and see me now as part of the All There Is – permeated with the All There Is – as it is with her?

I believe it is so. I believe she is more connected to me and to the universe now that she is not circumscribed by our world. I believe she moves in a broader brighter reality that cannot be understood in the womb world we know.

I believe she sees me and hears me and is part of me and part of the All There Is.

I know I see her and hear her every day – in birds and rainbows and newborn lambs black as a blank spot in the universe calling for their mama.

Let Me Be Dirt

The chimes on my porch sing the music of the wind, the music the wind has ever held and ever will. It is possible, I suppose, for one more gifted than I to transcribe this music into line-imprisoned ovals on paper, and from there to set it free again and sing it anew. Perhaps that is what composers do. Perhaps, in essence, that is all composers ever do. Perhaps that is all any of us ever do.

We take into ourselves of what is around us: sunlight, water, food, color, sound, affection; and thereby become what we are. And surely many other things are taken in as well: the daily news, the stock market report, the obituaries, the price of bread, crowding, loneliness, the cacophonies and the silences.

Are we, then, sponges? Or filters? Or sheets of glass that only allow the world to pass through or be shed off? Do we get to choose?

As for me, I hate the thought of being merely a sop, alternately soaked and dry, subject to vicissitudes, but ultimately never changed. And I think I lack the ability to be a filter, to choose what is worth holding back for myself, while deeming other things to be worthless and therefore let go. How would one choose? Isn't it likely the choices would change every day - that regret for what was discarded becomes the only constant the filter holds? Glass seems worst of all - never changed, even momentarily - oblivious, as well as nearly invisible, to its world. It is an existence that is non-existence - and its fragility bears witness to this fact.

I think there is another choice, a more natural choice. I think we can be dirt.

I love the idea of being dirt. I love thinking that I could be ground-down stones, no longer sharp and hard and unable to support life, that I could be the very old life of plants, and tiny animals, and large ones. I love it that warm sunlight and cool rains and the singing wind brings all things to the humble state of plain dirt. I love thinking that the glories of the world create, and re-create, the glories of the world through the humility, simplicity, complexity of plain dirt. I love it that all things become dirt and that dirt becomes all things.

Let me absorb the singing, the obituaries, the sunshine, all we know, and all we don't know.

Let me be dirt.

Planting Potatoes

It's time to dig my potatoes. We checked a couple weeks ago and there are lots of them – which is pretty exciting because we tried so many types and colors: reds, whites, golds, blues, rounds, oblongs and combinations. Just for fun. In addition to the potatoes.

Still, I like to get things right – inasmuch as that is possible. So, every year, at least since the advent of my access to the internet, I look up how to plant potatoes – in spite of the fact that I've planted them many years in the absence of that information resource. But is there a better way to grow potatoes? If so, I need to know what it is.

It's an odd thing. The search results, every year, are at once frustrating, depressing, and anxiety provoking. I want to do this thing right. I don't want to waste my efforts. I don't want to find out that I could have gotten twice the potatoes with half the work after it's too late to do it that way!

Potatoes have eyes. Let go long enough, these become nubs, then legs – or at least that's how they look. Bare, white, naked, twisted legs – which is the not the same as deformed because this is a natural thing for potatoes to do. Or at least that's how it appears to me.

The advice I read is that the perfect time to plant the seed potatoes is before the eyes have become nubs. Or after the eyes have become nubs. Don't bother to plant if they have legs. Or go ahead and plant with the legs (head start!) as long as you don't break them off. Or as long as you do break them off so new ones can sprout underground.

At any rate, when you cut the potatoes up so each eye can become a separate plant, be sure you do it a day or so ahead so the raw potato edges can dry and heal over a little. Or be sure you're ready to plant before you cut the potatoes up so they can be underground before the raw potato edges begin to dry.

Anyway, it's the planting itself that's critical. Potatoes should be planted underground in trenches. The trenches should be about six inches deep and the potatoes should be completely covered. Or the trenches should be about ten inches deep, the potatoes should be partially covered, and more dirt pulled up around the potatoes as the plants emerge. Or, build towers out of tires or buckets or barrels or pallets – and layer potatoes with dirt and straw in a repeating garden parfait – with radishes on top! Or you can just lay your potatoes on top of the ground – which has been carefully tilled and raked out smooth – and cover them with straw. Or you can skip the preparation, lay the potatoes on the ground – on the grass, on your yard – heck, on an old abandoned driveway – cover them with straw and walk away.

Any and all combinations of the foregoing strategies and methods are described – sometimes briefly, sometimes in detail – and nearly always accompanied by photographs of each step, the last photo showing a heap of successfully cultivated, delicious looking, ready to eat potatoes – as evidence of the validity, yes, even the superiority of that particular potato propagation scheme.

I've always assumed that the potato planting posts are intended to help people who have never planted potatoes, or to provide improved methods for experienced potato planters – sort of like potato evangelists showing people a new or better pathway.

So I read. Every year. And it's the same. Every year.

My thinking is that the first thing a person should try, in the absence of clear evidence in support of something else, is the easiest option – though, on occasion, if the evangelism is very compelling, I've given the more difficult plans a try.

This year, like most years, I found an out of the way spot where the soil is so poor nothing else will grow, but nonetheless a spot where there is good drainage and sunlight, and christened it the potato patch.

On the typical year, I spend an hour or two cutting up seed potatoes – some of which have eyes, some nubs; and a few have multiple legs of considerable length – depending upon when the potatoes were purchased; because I can't resist an interesting variety no matter when I happen upon it. If I cut up the potatoes early in the day, I'll plant immediately before the raw potato has a chance to dry. If I cut up the potatoes in the evening, I'll plant the next day after the raw potato has had a chance to heal over. Sometimes I'll start them in the evening and finish them up the next morning. I don't remember which of these took place this past spring.

I placed the potato chunks on the ground – which was either bare or supporting tiny tufts of grass – at more or less random distances apart from one another. I covered the whole area with several inches of straw, watered the straw down so it wouldn't blow away – and I was done.

Except for the praying. For most of my life I've prayed as easily, freely, and often as I've breathed. But lately, it's gotten harder. It's as if I've forgotten how. As if I've lost my way, as if I can't find a path I've walked a million times. What happened?

When I was ready for first grade, my mama discovered that our rural public school district had eight primary grades, two non-degreed teachers, one room, and no one who thought that was a problem. She declared her family henceforth to be devout Catholics and enrolled me in St. Mary's Elementary School. Even though she had been raised Baptist, she believed it was better to be well educated then religious – but I doubt she ever thought about it in exactly that way. It turned out that it wasn't an either/or kind of thing. I became, inevitably, both well educated and religious.

I loved the Church. Deeply. I did everything good Catholics are supposed to do – and tried to avoid those things good Catholics are not supposed to do – though the latter proved much more difficult than the former... I read everything I could, immersed myself in the liturgy, the tradition, the theology, the hagiography, the history. I prayed. Through the very best of Catholic teaching, I learned to meditate, to offer myself up unencumbered to the beauty and peace that is above me, around me, within me. Saint Francis de Sales led the way for me.

I was insatiable. I was also hurt. The Church rejected my gay son, my married and womanly aspirations for the priesthood, and my desire to end my childbearing capabilities. How could this be holy? How could it be loving? Indeed, could it even be considered good?

What else was there? Where else was I to go? Who else has found the sacred – and a way to touch it with their hands? Might there be a better way?

My search has become a joyful one. There are a million, billion ways to find the sacred and unite with it. Older ways. Newer ways. Ways marked with guideposts sufficiently close to one another to constitute a safety rail. Wandering ways that you mark on your own as you travel – if you so choose. I fell in love and I fell away – over and over again. I am enchanted and drawn by the Eastern religions – and have learned enough to know that I shouldn't lump them together in this way. I have found the gentleness too often hidden in the monotheistic traditions – and have learned enough to know that when they war, they are doing so as estranged brothers.

I have gathered pieces to myself, visions of other ways, as I've travelled their paths. I don't want to leave any of them behind. The paths crisscross one another, run side by side, veer in opposite directions, and cross again. Sometimes it's hard to tell one path from another. I'm convinced that it probably doesn't matter.

A few days ago a delivery person drove our long driveway to bring me a package. Seeing the concrete statues nestled in flower and herb gardens along the way, he felt safe to say, "I see you're Catholic!" I responded with the honesty that surprise statements often provoke, "I'm not sure anymore, but mostly I think I'm not."

"It sure looks like you're Catholic."

Indeed.

In my desperate moments, or moments that seem so, I feel the desperate need for prayer. When I am at work outdoors amongst the growing things, with the sunshine or the mists in the air, when life overwhelms me with its abundance or its power, I am irresistibly called to prayer. At the close of day, seeking clarity, calm, and peace, prayer beckons as the way.

What am I to do? I don't know the right way anymore.

But maybe it's as simple as planting potatoes. Perhaps there is no one way that's perfect for everybody. Maybe there are as many ways to plant potatoes as there are people planting them. Maybe people don't have to dedicate themselves to a single potato planting way. And maybe it's okay if they do. It might even be okay for them to think their way is the very best way of all ways. I don't know. What I do know is that if people follow their potato-planting way to the end, they'll likely end up with potatoes. I think it has much more to do with the nature of potatoes than the way they're planted.

Maybe a person should pray in the way they know – whatever way that is. If they find more than one way to pray, or not, it's okay. Because it's the nature of The Sacred that matters, not the way of the prayer.

So, am I Catholic? Well, that's how I pray – because it's the pathway I know best – not because it's the only pathway.

It's not too different from planting potatoes.

Shekinah in the Country

Now

Twilight settled on a day of season changing rain as the autumn of late summer gave way to the autumn of early winter. Steady it had come all day, and the slight breezes that shifted it swung from warm to cool. The river rose, the leaves fell, and the heart ached to walk in the colored mellow sunshine that was not to be for another year. But the rain beckoned, too.

Out into the cold and wet I walked, into rains, not the dreary gray of November, but hinting of them, warning that there was no time to lose, that this season of between-seasons would be but a moment. The leaves still colored lay loosely on the ground still green. The musty smell of the latter had not yet taken hold and the fresh smell of spring was a thing months in the past – or in the future. Yet there was no place to go. There was a call, but not of destination or even direction. It was a moment of change so captured, so clear, that it had become a restless stillness. It was a now, a now isolated from past and future, a pinpoint between them, rendering each indistinguishable from the other. I was called to walk, to move, but lacking perspective could only stand.

This moment, this instant, this now, held within it the green of summer, the color of fall, the chill of winter, and the wet of spring. It encompassed change and stillness as if they were one. And perhaps they are. Perhaps everything that ever was and everything that ever will be is encompassed in a full, round, directionless, vibrating now.

I saw that I am all I ever was and all I will ever be, and that I understood neither. I could see that time, and all things that happen in it, are as foolish and useless, as illusory and artificial as wandering aimlessly in a season-changing rain. It is better, far better, to simply stand and soak in the everything contained in the now.

Shekinah in the Country

About the Author

I am where I live.

There is a small curly black basalt bedded river in the north woods that, depending upon the season, rumbles, ripples, or glides its way to the coldest deepest lake on the continent. As rivers go, it is a youngster – fast, spirited, uneven, draining only the forest wilds, very unlike its older sand and silt bottomed brothers who flow sedately through cultivated fields, cities, and small woodlands. Yet, as all rivers are, it is timeless, here before I was here, before people were anywhere, here, doubtless, after all people are gone. The river responds to seasons as a child, exuberant in early spring and subdued by winter's cold, both reflecting and taking in all that surrounds and molds it. Thus, it is an old man, though not a mighty one, having witnessed seasons innumerable. Therefore, more than metaphor, it is the very moving sameness of time that is vast, and time that is not time at all. My young, old, ageless, timeless river. My neighbor.

In the summer, when the windows are open, I can hear its sighs and its songs. From my kitchen window, in late autumn, after the trees have lost their leaves, I can see its sparkle through the branches. Along its banks, deer drink and wolves hunt and eagles course the river path for fish and small prey. It is not possible to be sensate and unshaped by such a neighbor as my river.

There are no other neighbors visible from my home, no roads, no streetlights or yard lights, no mailboxes. Only the river and its world. There was no house at all till we built here, and we have tried to leave but a tiny mark on this world. Of our total acreage, we use less than ten percent, leaving those things that were here before us free to live peacefully with us. And they do. We have small barns and small flocks and folds, orchards and berry patches, vegetable gardens, and herb gardens.

If ever there was an Eden, this is it. But Eden and Paradise were not at all the same. Bad and puzzling things can happen in a garden, even an unspoiled beautiful one.

Since I was nineteen, this is what I've wanted. I saw it in a dream. I see it as a dream. It carries me, as it always has. I carry it, as I always have. It is within me. It surrounds me. It is me.

www.ingramcontent.com/pod-product-compliance
Lightning Source LLC
Chambersburg PA
CBHW071308040426
42444CB00009B/1921